Pet Owner's Guide to the
ENGLISH SPRINGER SPANIEL

Don Miller

RINGPRESS

RINGPRESS

Published by Ringpress Books,
Vincent Lane, Dorking, Surrey,
RH4 3YX, England.

First Published 1995
This edition reprinted 1997
© Interpet Publishing.
All rights reserved

ISBN 1 86054 020 1

Printed in Hong Kong through Printworks Int. Ltd.

Contents

The English Springer Spaniel is the most effective all-purpose gundog, a glamorous show dog, and an ideal family companion.

This book is dedicated to Jack, Morag, and the late Meg Bolton, whose Pencloe Springers introduced me to the breed.

About the author

Don Miller has bred and owned English Springer Spaniels for over thirty years, and with his wife, Jenny, runs a successful boarding kennels, situated high on the Chiltern Hills in rural Hertfordshire. They have now bred eleven Champions, and their prefix Feorlig is in demand worldwide. Don is an International Championship Show judge and has been to Sweden, Finland, Holland and Ireland on judging appointments. In 1987 he had the honour of judging English Springers at Crufts. Don is also passed to award Challenge Certificates in Welsh Springer Spaniels and American Cocker Spaniels.

On the administrative side, Don was Secretary of the Southern English Springer Spaniel Club for ten years, and is now President. He is also Chairman of the ESS Welfare organisation. He is also breed correspondent of Britain's weekly newspaper, *Dog World.*

Photographs by Carol Ann Johnson

Chapter One

INTRODUCING THE ENGLISH SPRINGER SPANIEL

EARLY HISTORY

The origins of the English Springer Spaniel are somewhat obscure, but it is generally agreed that, like all our Spaniel breeds, their first home was Spain, imported by the Roman legions during their occupation. The actual term of 'Springer' was introduced around 1570 when Dr Caius, physician to Edward VI, was writing on dogs and used the term to describe all Land Spaniels.

In the late 17th century the flintlock gun was introduced into Britain, making it possible for sportsmen to engage in 'flying shooting' – and this was the start of fine gundog training. Obviously, any attempt to shoot over wild, uncontrolled Spaniels with any sort of gun would have been as useless then as now. As a consequence, over the next three hundred years, Spaniels were transformed from untrained, wild beaters, to smooth, polished gundogs who could hunt within gun range, and retrieve with a tender mouth, in order to save the game for the table.

The Springer has come to the fore to rank as the world's most effective all-round gundog, with the ability to spring the game, and to work as a natural hunter, coupled with the excellent qualities of a water dog and retriever.

Around 1800 the first pure strain of English Springers was developed by the Boughey family of Aqualate in Shropshire, who bred from their strain of Spaniel very carefully, keeping a stud book from 1813 onwards. This strain was kept in successive generations of the family for over a century. In 1903 the Boughey family bred Field Trial Champion Velox Powder, whose pedigree goes back to the Aqualate Stud Book and to Mop 1, who was whelped in 1812.

The first Field Trial was held in Derbyshire in 1899, but Springers were not in the awards – so different from today when English Springers tend to dominate such trials.

OFFICIAL RECOGNITION

It was not until 1902 that the Kennel Club recognised the English Springer as a specific variety of Spaniel and gave the breed a separate classification. The first Springer Field Champion in the world was Rivington Sam, whose blood still flows through the veins of many present-day Springers. It was generally acknowledged that Sam was a first cross between a Cocker and a English Setter, and over the years, outcross blood of breeds such as the Clumber Spaniel, the Irish Setter, and the Field Spaniel was introduced. This had some advantages, such as improving heads, but, fortunately, the Springer emerged as an entirely distinctive breed, and in the modern show ring the English Springer can more than hold its own.

However, the early dogs were much of a mixed bag and when English and Welsh Springers were given recognition as separate breeds in 1902, registration was purely on the basis of appearance. Many dogs were registered with doubtful pedigrees, and some with no pedigree at all. As a general rule, if the dog was red-and-white, it was registered as a Welsh Springer, and if it was liver-and-white, it was classed as an English Springer, although a number of other physical characteristics would also have separated the breeds.

THE BREED DEVELOPS
In 1903 the Kennel Club offered a class specially for English Springers at their show, and in 1906 the liver-and-white dog Beechgrove Will was made the first Champion in the breed, and Fansom became the first Champion bitch.

The English Springer Spaniel Club was founded in 1921, and since then a network of clubs has been established to accommodate the increasing popularity of the breed as a working and show dog.

In the USA the American Spaniel Club was founded in 1880, and its task was to attempt to classify the different Spaniel breeds. It was decided that this should be done by size, and all Spaniels over 28lbs were classified as Springers. The first English Springer Spaniel was registered in 1910. In 1924 the English Springer Spaniel Association was formed, and the breed started to increase in popularity. In 1927 the English Springer Spaniel Field Trial Association became the parent club for the breed.

THE ENGLISH SPRINGER TODAY
Anyone seeking a shooting companion should look no further than the English Springer, as he has no superior among the Spaniel breeds as a worker. A well-trained Springer is a joy to work with; he is the jack of all trades and master of them all. In the show ring, we now have one of the world's most attractive breeds and with continued success, the rewards of breeding true and to type are now evident.

The English Springer is an ideal family dog, and absolutely adores children. This is a dog that has a combination of all the canine virtues, and none of the vices attributed to some breeds. A highly intelligent, much-admired breed, with the friendliest of dispositions, the Springer has endeared itself to dog lovers worldwide.

The breed has attracted media attention, and Springers are now used on billboards, in TV commercials, and on advertisements to promote the sales of many products including, of course, dog foods. They are also featured on a

This is a breed that loves children, and will be a welcome addition to any family.

A well-trained English Springer is a joy to work with.

The English Springer Spaniel is among the most attractive of all the breeds, and is always much admired at dog shows.

wide variety of greeting cards and postcards. In Britain the English Springer is never out of the top ten most popular breeds, based on registrations with the Kennel Club. In America, the Springer also has a huge following and features in the top twenty breeds, compiled by the American Kennel Club. The Springer has also gained ground in Canada, Australia, New Zealand, Scandinavia and the rest of Europe, and with the import restrictions now relaxed in Iceland, it is the most popular breed on the island – living proof that the English Springer adapts to all climates.

The breed can be seen in all walks of life. President George Bush and Barbara doted on their working type, Millie, who went on to publish a bestseller entitled *Millie's Book*, a tale of her life in the White House, which grossed over half a million dollars in royalties! HM Queen Elizabeth II takes a great interest in the Sandringham strain of English Springers, who are very successful in Field and Working Trials.

THE VERSATILE ENGLISH SPRINGER
The adaptability of the English Springer is never more evident than in modern society. With its hunting instinct and keen sense of smell, the breed is in great demand by Customs and Excise as drug detection or 'sniffer dogs'. With the drugs problem increasing in prisons, the Prison Service is now using English Springers for detection purposes, with successful results. They are also used to detect illegal immigrants in containers and holds of ships. The armed forces have recruited Springers to detect arms or munitions.

The gentle and biddable temperament of the Springer has made it much in demand as a therapy dog. This entails visits to hospitals and residential homes for the elderly, and the dogs act as a great morale booster, and have even been an aid to recovery in some instances. Hearing Dogs for the Deaf is a new role that the breed has adapted to, with excellent results. Specifically trained to be attracted by noises, such as the doorbell, the telephone, etc., the dog alerts the owner, bringing the relevant noise to their attention.

The English Springer is a highly intelligent dog, and can be trained to compete in Obedience, Agility and Working Trials. For those who have an active lifestyle, and who want to get the most from their dog, the English Springer stands out as the all-round canine companion.

Chapter Two
CHOOSING A PUPPY

In my experience, the prospective purchaser of an English Springer puppy will be seeking a family companion first and foremost. Although puppies may be obtained for the purpose of work or show, primarily the Springer craves companionship, and it is of the utmost importance that the dog enters the home to spend a lifetime as a family pet.

So, having decided that the English Springer is the right breed for you, the next stage is to embark on the exciting quest of seeking your ideal dog. However, there are several factors to be considered before contacting reputable breeders.

WORK OR SHOW TYPE
If you are acquiring the Springer as a shooting companion, it is imperative that you contact an established breeder of working type, with a proven working pedigree in the background. The modern Field Trial Springer can be extremely hyper-active, although also very biddable and easy to train. However, I would not recommend a working type as a family companion. They tend to be too exuberant, and the lack of exercise, coupled with the loss of the work the dog has been bred for, can lead to frustration and often to a change in temperament.

If you want to get involved in showing your Springer, you should go to a reputable show kennel. The best way of choosing a kennel is to attend a show where there are classes for English Springers. In the catalogue, highlight the dogs that you admire, and if your selections favour the same breeding line, then that is the breeder to contact. The show Springer has a more gentle and docile character, and so this type is ideally suited to the family environment.

DOG OR BITCH
Once you have decided on the type of Springer you want, the next step will be to decide whether to have a dog or a bitch. There are pros and cons for both, so let us consider them. At present, the demand is for bitches, possibly because there are owners who think they may want to breed from their pet at some stage. There is also the mistaken belief that bitches are more faithful than dogs. This old wives' tale has no truth, as the Springer male can be more faithful,

If you plan to show your Springer, make sure you go to a reputable show kennel.

English Springers can be black and white, as well as the liver and white colour which is more commonly seen.

The working English Springer is a very active dog, and a dog from these bloodlines will become frustrated if he is not given a job of work to do.

loving and gentle in comparison to bitches, who can be very independent.

A male is the natural choice for the hunter, as no days will be lost for shooting due to the bitch's twice-yearly, three week season. On the other hand, you may acquire an over-sexed male, who will develop the wanderlust when bitches in the neighbourhood come into season. There is, of course, the option to neuter, which is applicable to both dogs and bitches. This is a personal decision for the owner to make.

COLOUR

It can be a surprise to newcomers to the breed that the Springer can be other colours, and not just liver-and-white, which is most generally seen. Any recognised Land Spaniel colour is acceptable, but liver-and-white, black-and-white, or either of these colours with tan markings, are preferred. The only colour not desired is the red of the Welsh Springer Spaniel.

I have bred all of the recognised colours, and I find the liver-and-white with deep, rich tan markings, can be most attractive. The tri-colour or black-and-white with tan can be a very appealing combination. The black-and-white is fast gaining in popularity, and if the dog is kept in the peak of condition, you cannot better the texture, condition and shine on a black-and-white's coat. This is in comparison to a liver-and-white who, after a warm summer, can look decidedly bleached. Markings should not be of consideration in the show ring, but I have found that the prospective exhibitor will always select an evenly marked puppy with a good blaze on the head. For working purposes, it seems the general rule of the whiter the better, as the dog can be easily seen in the fields or stubble. Markings should be of little consequence to the pet owner, as the main consideration must be temperament and suitability to the home.

Genetically, colour can be quite a minefield. In a recent hearing at the English Kennel Club, a leading geneticist stated that it was an impossibility to breed a black-and-white from generations of liver-and-whites. Accepted by the Kennel Club, this ruling has been fiercely contested by many experienced breeders.

TAIL DOCKING

It is generally accepted that Springers are docked. However, in Britain a law has been passed prohibiting a lay person from docking, but still permitting veterinarians to carry out the practice. We therefore have the situation where we have docked and undocked litters available. The Breed Standard states that the tail is customarily docked and, if docked, it is about one third of the tail removed within three days of birth. I have always found this to be a painless procedure. Docking has been banned in several Scandinavian countries and elsewhere in Europe. Docked or undocked – the choice is yours.

THE OLDER DOG

The demands and suitability of an older dog are dependent on the responsible attitude and circumstances of a prospective owner. For those who are out at work for some periods during the day, the older dog can be an ideal choice. The elderly owner will also appreciate the mature dog in comparison to a boisterous puppy, who needs so much attention and can be a danger to the physically infirm. You will be acquiring a tailor-made Springer who will be healthy, well-mannered, inoculated, and eager to become part of a new family. Older dogs can be acquired through welfare or rescue organisations, and sometimes breeders will have adult dogs available for rehoming. There can be various reasons for this: a dog may have failed to reach show potential, or may have developed ring-shyness. Breeding stock can also become available, as a bitch cannot be bred from after eight years of age, and sometimes stud dogs are no longer required.

It is important to bear in mind that you are acquiring a kennel dog, and so it may be several weeks before the dog or bitch adapts to being clean in the house. I have always felt a great sense of loyalty to my oldies and have never wanted to part with them, but, over the years, I have been cajoled by friends to part with a few. It is consolation to know that the rest of their days will be spent in comfort and companionship, cared for by a loving owner.

FINDING A BREEDER
Now that you are aware of your requirements, it is essential to buy from a suitable and reputable breeder. If you do not know an English Springer breeder, it is advisable to contact your national Kennel Club, where a register of recognised breeders in all breeds is available. You will be forwarded a list of breeders and also details of the breed clubs. The breed club secretary will often know of puppies that are available or litters that are due, and will be able to guide you in the right direction.

Other avenues that you can explore are advertisements in the dog papers and magazines, and there are several companies that specialise in compiling puppy registers from established breeders. When you contact a breeder, be prepared for something of a grilling, as you will have to satisfy the breeder that you will be a suitable Springer owner. Breeders have ground rules regarding the placement of their puppies, and if you do not have the lifestyle to suit an English Springer, you may be met with a polite refusal.

If you are fortunate to find a litter at an early age, it may be possible to follow their progress from the age of two weeks through the formative period, until they are ready to leave the nest at eight weeks old. Hopefully, on your initial meeting with the breeder, you will have formed a mutual rapport. Ideally, this is the opportunity for you to clarify all conditions regarding the purchase of your puppy. Gone are the days when a male cost less than a bitch – it takes the same amount of care, feeding and attention.

Do not alienate the breeder by trying to barter over the price of the puppy, as this will not go down well! Some breeders sell puppies on 'breeding terms', which may mean retaining the breeding rights on a bitch, or retaining the stud

All puppies are appealing. In the case of the English Springer, the puppy should look like a miniature of the finished article.

Temperament is the most important consideration when selecting a dog. These Springer puppies already show the friendly, confident disposition which is a hallmark of the breed.

When you go to choose your puppy, it is helpful if you can see the mother, and, if possible, the father, so you can get some idea of how the puppies will turn out.

rights on a dog. These arrangements are fraught with problems, and you should not enter into them, unless you fully understand what is involved, and there is a signed agreement on both sides.

You will certainly see the dam of the litter, and maybe the sire if he lives on the premises. This will give you a good idea as to how your puppy may mature. If the sire is not available, the breeder will be able to inform you of his whereabouts and you may be able to make arrangements to see him.

ASSESSING THE PUPPIES
Although you may have been lucky to see the puppies through their various stages of development, it is not until seven or eight weeks that their little characters blossom. When choosing a puppy, bear in mind that, in the Springer, you are looking at a miniature of the finished article.

Stand the puppy on a table and look for a solid, well-boned and compact puppy. The head should show promise of a good muzzle, of a good length, and with a marked stop (the step up between the muzzle and the skull). The eyes should be dark, although a Springer's eyes will darken with age. The puppy should also have a good, level topline, a well-set tail, and well-developed quarters. The coat is an important indicator to the puppy's general condition, and it should be flat and clean. If it is dry and scaly, and the puppy is scratching, it could indicate fleas, lice or even worm infestation.

Ideally, you will be looking for a bold puppy, who will be confident and approach you looking for the fuss expected from humans. Sometimes you will find a puppy who stands aloof from the others – this will probably be the breeder's choice as it considers itself above the others and may be the future Champion! If there is a slightly nervous puppy, then the suitability of the new home is important. It can be beneficial if this type of puppy is placed on a one-to-one basis, or with an older couple. I never choose a puppy for prospective owners, although I offer advice on the differences of each member of the litter. I find that a puppy will normally seek out its new owner.

PREPARATIONS
Before collecting your puppy, it is a good idea to ask the breeder for a copy of the diet chart of the feeding routine. It is vital that you adhere to this routine, as any change could lead to a very sick puppy. In accordance with the diet chart, you can stock up with the recommended foods and supplements. Also in preparation, you can find a bed. Normally a cardboard box, lined with old clothes or fleece polyester bedding, is quite sufficient for the first few weeks. You will also need to buy feeding and water bowls.

COLLECTING YOUR PUPPY
When you collect your puppy, be prepared for the journey home, and go equipped with a washing-up bowl, lots of old newspapers and a towel in case he is sick in the car. A good indication of your puppy's intention to be sick is

continuous yawning. Try to collect your puppy at the weekend, preferably early on, so that you have plenty of time to settle him in when most of the family are at home. The breeder will give you a receipt for your payment, a certificate of pedigree, a diet chart (if not already received) and a Kennel Club registration application certificate. You will then have to complete the paperwork for transfer of ownership. You should also be informed of the worming programme the puppy has undergone, and whether he has been inoculated. In most cases, the inoculation course starts at around eight or twelve weeks of age.

ARRIVING HOME
It is now time for your puppy to face the brave, new world and, although this can be a traumatic experience, it can be made relatively painless with some common sense and a sympathetic approach.

On arrival, introduce the puppy to the garden (yard), where, hopefully, he will relieve himself. This should be greeted with a great deal of praise. The puppy will probably feel rather tired and forlorn. The best plan is to offer a bowl of powdered milk, laced with a teaspoonful of glucose powder. If you have travelled a distance, the puppy is unlikely to have been fed for quite a period of time, so make him a meal according to the breeder's instructions. It is important to have fresh water available at all times.

I am working on the assumption that the puppy is to be the one dog in the family, so an outside kennel is deemed unnecessary. For a house dog, the kitchen is usually delegated as the puppy's sleeping quarters. As puppies can be destructive, it is advisable to opt for an improvised bed, and this can be a clean cardboard box, with a side cut out, and the bottom layered with newspapers, covered with some of the family's old garments. Try to keep the bed away from draughts and damp and ensure that all electric wires and toxic liquids are out of the puppy's reach.

It is inevitable that hordes of friends and relatives will descend upon you to greet the new arrival. However, a puppy, like a human baby, needs a great deal of sleep and quiet, and children, especially, must be taught that a resting puppy must never be disturbed. If a puppy is continually woken, it can develop into a nervous and irritable youngster.

THE FIRST NIGHT
A lonely puppy, separated from his siblings, will probably give you a couple of sleepless nights. Be patient, and try to comfort the puppy by leaving an old alarm clock ticking, or a radio playing soft music. A well-wrapped hot-water bottle can also help. Try not to relent and take the puppy to the bedroom, as he will consider this to be his haven for the rest of his life! Before retiring, line the kitchen floor with newspapers for the inevitable accidents, and, remember, a dog is a creature of habit. If you get up 5a.m., and let the puppy out to relieve himself, you will live to regret it!

It is essential to provide a well-balanced diet to ensure your English Springer will develop into a healthy, active dog.

Chapter Three
CARING FOR YOUR PUPPY

FEEDING

Regardless of whether you have bought your puppy for work, show, or purely as a companion dog, it is essential to give the correct diet in the early days, as good food will promote good bone, and your puppy will grow into a healthy, active dog. The breeder has laid the groundwork for you, with a detailed feed chart, and it is advisable not to change the routine or the type of food to begin with. A young puppy settling into a new home is very vulnerable, and so you do not want to cause any further upset, particularly a dietary change which may result in sickness or diarrhoea. If, for some reason, you have to change the food, this must be done gradually, mixing in the new food, bit by bit, so the puppy has a chance to adapt to the change.

The dog is a natural carnivore – a meat-eater, so I wean my puppies on a proprietary brand of canned puppy meat before introducing them to meat. Your puppy will probably be used to powdered milk, so keep to this routine, gradually mixing in some cow's milk. When my puppies are eight weeks old, and ready to leave home, they are on five meals a day, and this will continue until they are three months old. My feeding chart for puppies up to three months old is as follows:

BREAKFAST (8a.m.): Cereal or puppy meal, mixed in half a pint of warm, powdered milk. Add half a teaspoon of glucose. A raw egg can be mixed in once a day.
LUNCH (12 noon): 8-12ozs finely chopped meat. Add a handful of puppy meal, and a crushed calcium tablet with vitamin D. Include added vitamins. Meat can be cooked, raw, or canned, or fish can be fed.
SNACK (3p.m.) As breakfast, but instead of milk, add half a can of rice pudding, or custard can also be used.
SUPPER (6p.m.) As lunch, but omit all additives. A small amount of cod-liver oil can be added occasionally.
BEDTIME: A bowl of milk and some small biscuits.

THE GROWING PUPPY

Up to six months of age, decrease the number of meals to three per day with the quantities being increased. This is achieved by eliminating some of the milk feeds, so the diet will be:

BREAKFAST: A meat meal.
MIDDAY: A milk meal at midday,using cow's milk.
SUPPER: A meat meal.

The transition to nine months of age means a reduction to two meals a day: a milk meal for breakfast and meat meal late afternoon. From nine months onwards, you should be feeding one meal a day consisting of one and a quarter pounds of meat and a couple of handfuls of wholemeal biscuit, normally fed early evening. Calcium tablets with vitamin D, glucose, and cod-liver oil can be obtained from any good pharmacy, and are essential to promote calcium and phosphorus in growing puppies.

I am not a great lover of complete foods, but in modern society they are convenient and, according to the manufacturers' claims, they include all the nutrients required for a healthy dog. You must ensure that you read all the instructions regarding the feeding of complete food, and you must have fresh water available at all times. If you are feeding fresh meat which is refrigerated, then it must be removed before you feed and allowed to warm to room temperature.

THE FUSSY FEEDER
Springers are normally good eaters, so do not be concerned if your puppy only toys with his food for the few days after he arrives home. He is missing the competition of his littermates. Take the food away and wait until the next mealtime. If the behaviour continues, then the onus is on you to encourage the puppy to eat. This can entail hand-feeding, which requires a great deal of patience and can also cause you a lot of frustration. The breakthrough may not come for a couple of months, but your efforts will be rewarded with a happy, healthy dog. By all means, give your puppy tidbits, but beware of high-protein foods such as cheese and goat's milk – I have seen Springers who developed an allergy to such food.

HOUSE-TRAINING
House-training need not be a problem if you use kindness and a sensible approach. Always remember that prevention is better than cure. After a sleep or meal, take your puppy outdoors and supervise until he relieves himself. If he performs, then give plenty of praise. Springer puppies are normally very clean and respond quickly to praise and encouragement.

Do not expect miracles within a couple of days, as a puppy can answer nature's calls a multitude of times during the day. If an accident does occur in the house, it is simply unkind to scold or rub his nose in it – a puppy does not know he has done wrong unless he is caught in the act. In general, a Springer puppy will be house-trained in ten to fourteen days, although it is still advisable to cover the floor of the sleeping quarters with newspapers during the night.

HOUSING

It is advisable that the purchase of an expensive dog bed be delayed until your puppy has finished teething. This could be when he is approaching his first birthday. A variety of dog beds are on offer. Personally, I would reject the traditional wicker basket, which can be easily destroyed and can also harbour dirt. My own favourite is the hard, plastic moulded bed, lined with fleece polyester bedding or a washable dog duvet. There is also the bean bag, which is extremely comfortable, but woe betide if a sharp claw tears the covering – you will be sweeping up granules for the next few months!

Many breeders also use and recommend a crate as the dog's sleeping quarters. These may be made of wood, processed fibreglass, metal or wire. A crate affords the dog privacy in the home, and provides a safe means of travel.

OUTSIDE KENNELS

Thankfully, the old tradition of a small kennel, with a dog chained to it, has disappeared. Nowadays, you can purchase high-quality, spacious kennels and runs, that are manufactured to provide comfortable and hygienic accommodation. It is a good idea to concrete an area to accommodate the kennel and run. A roofed run can protect your dog during a rainy period, and can also provide shade during a hot summer.

You can also improvise by using part of a garage or shed, but the buildings must be dry, light, airy, and free from draughts. Always remember that the Springer craves companionship, so site the kennel where he can see activity and can receive some personal attention.

TOYS

Toys are part of a puppy's upbringing, and as a Springer puppy can be particularly destructive, it is vital that the toys are safe. I advise against the pull-and-tug toys, which I particularly dislike. This type of toy can seriously damage your puppy's dentition and jaw formation. Squeaky toys are fine, provided the squeaker has been removed, as, if it is swallowed, you may have to resort to surgery.

Very small balls can be lethal, but a large bouncy ball can last for years. Rawhide bones, chews, etc. are excellent for your puppy's teeth. Homemade toys, such as the tubes of toilet-rolls and kitchen-towel rolls, and empty cardboard boxes, can give your puppy endless hours of fun.

WORMING

A good breeder will have carried out a worming programme on your puppy, and will inform you when the next dosage is due. Although the dam will have been wormed and your puppy will have been given treatment at least three

As your Springer gets older, you should reduce the number of meals, and so by nine months of age you should be feeding one meal a day.

ABOVE: A plastic, moulded bed, fitted with comfortable bedding, is the most suitable for a Springer Spaniel puppy.

BELOW: There are many different types of dog bed available.

times, the wormer may not catch eggs, which will mean that worms will hatch. Therefore, worming has to be carried out regularly after you obtain the puppy.

Generally, the most common worms to be found in dogs are roundworms and tapeworms. It is roundworms that normally affect puppies and in-whelp bitches. Worming should be carried out when your puppy is three months old, and then every three months until he is a year old. Thereafter, your Springer should be wormed on an annual basis, unless you see signs of infestation.

Worming treatments can be obtained from your vet, and these are available in all palatable forms – paste, tablets and powders. It is important to use the treatment as directed, and give the correct dosage according to your dog's weight. If, after treatment, you see evidence of worms, hygiene is of the utmost importance. The stools must be disposed of safely, and then your hands will need to be well scrubbed. Do not allow children near the puppy at this time.

Tapeworms are normally found in the adult dog. These can be recognised as white segments joined together, and they are usually found on the tail or rear feathering. If tapeworm is to be eliminated, the head, embedded in the intestine, must be destroyed or it will grow again. A safe worming agent from your vet will be required. Worming is essential to the health and well-being of your pet. If infestation is severe, your dog will be listless, he will gain no nourishment from food, he will develop bad breath and will cough. I have even seen a puppy suffer a fit, which has been caused by worms.

INOCULATIONS
Your puppy will be ready for inoculations at nine to ten weeks, depending on your vet's policy, and the prevalence of canine diseases in your area. The inoculations will protect your puppy against the main diseases of distemper, two types of leptospirosis, canine viral hepatitis and parvovirus. Until the course of injections is completed, you must confine your puppy to the house and garden, and he must not frequent places used by other dogs or come into contact with them.

It never ceases to amaze me why vets expect an unprotected puppy to sit in a waiting room with other animals that could well be harbouring contagious diseases. Leave your puppy in the car until you are summoned, and then carry him into the treatment room. The first inoculation is followed, two weeks later by a second injection to complete the course. The inoculation will last for a year, and from then on, your Springer must have an annual booster.

After the second injection, you may be informed that it is safe for the puppy to leave the house and go for walks. However, I always wait for a couple of weeks to allow immunity to build up.

Another inoculation that is available offers protection against kennel cough. This can be invaluable if you need to use boarding kennels at any time. A nasal inoculation must be administered five days before your dog goes into kennels. The inoculation lasts for a period of nine months, but with so many strains of cough it can only protect your dog against some of them.

Keep your inoculation card in a safe place, as no reputable boarding kennels will take in a dog unless it has a current inoculation certificate.

LEAD TRAINING

After an initial settling in period, and while your puppy is between inoculations, it is a good idea to initiate your puppy into walking on a lead. This may sound quite simple, but a rebellious, energetic little puppy can prove to be a handful.

It is pointless to purchase an expensive leather collar, as your Springer will soon grow out of it. I suggest buying a cheap, nylon slip collar and a lead about four feet long. Accustom the puppy to wearing the collar, but take it off at intervals and also during the night, as it will mark the hair on the neck. This will create a bad impression in the ring if you are intending to show your dog. Many puppies find the collar quite irritating at first, but most will quickly learn to accept it.

When your puppy is used to wearing a collar, you can attach the lead. Start off by letting your puppy wander around the garden and house to get used to this strange extension. Make sure your puppy is supervised during these sessions, or he will get hopelessly tangled up! On your first venture outdoors, you will probably find that your puppy will go through all the stock tricks of the trade – bucking, rearing, pulling and digging his heels in. This will give you the opportunity to teach your puppy his name, and to give lots of praise and encouragement. It is always useful to have some treats on hand as enticements, and with patience, coupled with lots of praise, you will find that your puppy will soon walk properly, and the exercise will be associated with something enjoyable. Always walk your dog on the left-hand side, as this will benefit you in the conformation and obedience rings.

When your puppy is a little older, I would recommend a choke-chain or check-chain, as I prefer to call it. If used properly, with the chain running through the top of the ring, it will release automatically and, therefore, give you more control by checking movements.

EXERCISE

Recent evidence suggests that over-exercising a puppy can lead to hip dysplasia on reaching maturity. This is a condition where the head of the femur (long leg bone) is out of shape and will not fit in the socket of the pelvis. A puppy's bone conformation is soft and immature, and so damage can occur. Although you may be tempted to take your puppy out for long walks, you must curtail the amount of exercise, using your own common sense. It is also important to prevent your puppy from running up and down stairs, as this could cause his elbows to go out.

After your puppy has been inoculated, he may be taken for short walks on the lead. Up until ten months old, gentle strolls are in order. During this period, you can get your puppy used to travelling in the car, and you should visit town centres, so you can get him socialised and acclimatised to traffic

An indoor crate is an invaluable item of equipment, as long as your puppy is not confined for long periods. It is particularly useful when you take your Springer out in the car.

Puppies are used to curling up and sleeping together, and it is inevitable that your puppy will miss the warmth and companionship of his littermates for the first few nights in his new home.

Correct: If a check-chain is put on correctly, with the chain running through the top of the ring, it is a useful aid for training.

Incorrect: A check-chain that is put on incorrectly cannot release automatically.

noise. During exercise, make sure you are a responsible dog owner, and clean up after your dog. Never let your dog off the lead near a road, and keep him under control near farms where livestock are in the fields.

GOOD MANNERS

Ask any Springer owner if there can be such a creature as a well-mannered Springer, and you will receive a quizzical look! Springers are champion 'ssnack-snitchers' and all owners have an extra sense to contend with this. However, you can have a well-mannered Springer if you teach him to behave from puppyhood.

Be firm and never give tidbits from the table. If you do not want your Springer to get on the furniture, this must be instilled into your puppy right from the start. It is your duty as an owner to lay the foundation and to prevent your dog from acquiring bad habits. You may find that your puppy is possessive towards his food or toys, and shows aggressive tendencies. This behaviour must be nipped in the bud, especially if there are children in the house.

Chapter Four
TRAINING YOUR SPRINGER

WHERE TO START

Basic obedience training is essential for the Springer in order for the pet owner to have a happy relationship with the dog. There are many local Obedience clubs, which are usually advertised locally. In most instances, your vet will have information of what is going on in your area.

The potential gundog requires elementary obedience, as he is useless until he obeys your commands. In fact, it is more often the owner who needs the training, not the dog, and many a promising worker has been ruined by an inexperienced handler. Anyone who wants to get involved in gundog training would be well advised to contact a local gundog club. Here you will benefit from the expertise of experienced and knowledgeable trainers.

The show fraternity does very little obedience training, as a different discipline is required in the show ring.

The early stages of obedience training can commence at home. It is essential to bear in mind that during training sessions you must be patient, firm, encouraging, and lavish in your praise. Training a puppy must always be associated with lots of fuss and little chastisement. All of the basic exercises should develop into pleasurable activities for your puppy, so restrict training sessions to five minutes work daily, as a young puppy will quickly become bored and lose interest.

The first step is to get your puppy used to responding to his name. This is a very easy lesson to teach, as your puppy will be only too keen to come to you if you are offering food or a game. Make sure you always sound excited, so that your puppy cannot wait to come rushing up to you!

SIT

This is a simple exercise, and, if it is easily mastered, it should give you the pride and enthusiasm to tackle more difficult tasks. Start by putting your right hand under your puppy's chin, and gently press down on the rump with your left hand. At the same time, lift the puppy's head, giving the command "Sit". He will now be in a sitting position, and you can hold him there for a second or two.

As you progress, the exercise should be taught giving the command "Sit",

LEFT: Apply gentle pressure on the hindquarters when teaching the Sit.

BELOW: The Down is a natural position for a dog, and so it should be easy to learn. At a later stage it can be incorporated with the Stay exercise.

When teaching the Stay exercise, build up your distance gradually. Resist the temptation of progressing too quickly – if your dog does not have the opportunity to make mistakes, he will learn the exercise far more quickly.

and raising your left hand. Finish the exercise with a different tone of voice and plenty of praise. Repeat this lesson five or six times, giving him short breaks between the exercise – always remembering to give plenty of praise. Repeat the lessons twice a day, and soon the puppy will be sitting automatically as soon as you give the command.

HEELWORK

Lead training should now be well underway (See Chapter Two). The art of walking to heel is simply an extension of this exercise, with the added benefit that you have far greater control over your puppy. This is essential when you take your dog out in a busy urban environment.

For heelwork training, I prefer to use a check-chain. This is a useful aid to training, as long as it is worn correctly. The chain must run through the top of the ring so that it releases automatically. The object of the exercise is to have the pup walking by your side, with his head level with your left leg. In most cases, the pup will run ahead and pull. If this happens, give the command "Heel", accompanied by a jerk on the lead to bring the puppy back to heel. The check-chain will release the second you have jerked the lead, so the puppy is in no discomfort; it just serves to reinforce the lesson.

Maintain pressure on the lead so that the pup walks in the heel position for several minutes. The lead should be allowed to slacken and the correction procedure continued. The lessons should be repeated twice a day, with variations of about-turns, and left and right turns.

DOWN

This is an exercise your puppy should learn easily, as the Down is a natural position for the dog. It is useful in a variety of situations, and a quick response to the command could save a dog's life in an emergency.

Start with your puppy in the Sit position. Give the command "Down", at the same time lifting his forepaws into a prone position. Apply slight downward pressure on the lead as you place him in position. Any attempt to rise must be discouraged by showing him the flat of the hand and giving the command.

Continue the exercise daily, increasing the time the dog is kept in position. The exercise is invaluable if you intend to work your Springer, as, with progress, you will be able to 'drop' him, which makes it more difficult for him to 'run in' or 'chase'.

STAY

When your dog is put in the Sit position, he should not get up until he is told to do so. This is where the Stay exercise comes into force.

Put the puppy on a lead, give the command "Sit", followed by the command "Stay". Hold your puppy in this position with the left hand and, simultaneously, make a positive downward movement, with your right hand, in front of his nose. Give plenty of praise, and then let your puppy have a little run to relax. Repeat the exercise daily, gradually walking three or four steps away from your puppy, still holding the lead, and then returning to his side. When you have accomplished this, you can then move in front of the dog dropping the lead and leaving him in the Sit position. Ultimately, when your puppy has mastered the Sit and the Stay, you will be able to increase the distances until you can leave him – even when you are out of sight

RECALL

Early training for your puppy should consist of encouraging the puppy to respond to the command "Come", coupled with the frequent use of his name. This can be achieved by squatting down to the pup's level and giving a cajoling command – "Rover, Come". This can be accompanied by outstretched arms to encourage the puppy to come to your lap for his reward of fuss and attention.

The next step is to put your puppy on a lead in the Sit, and give the command "Stay". Walk away to about the length of the lead, and call "Come". Giving lots of encouragement, gently pull the puppy towards you. Gradually lengthen the lead with cord or string until the puppy shows reliability. The ultimate in this exercise is when the puppy comes to you without the assistance of the lead.

MAKING PROGRESS

The Springer is a dog of great intelligence, who is very biddable and sweet-natured, so, in your training, the first virtue is patience. While repetition is the key to responsive work, there must be the constant reward of praise. Above all, avoid boredom and make the sessions enjoyable for the puppy.

TRAINING TARGETS

The English Springer is the most versatile of gundogs. The breed is considered to be the all-rounder of the working fraternity, at the same time adapting to the role of a loved family companion. Basic obedience may satisfy the pet owner, but others may wish to progress further in Obedience or Agility competition. If you are a working enthusiast, you may wish to further your dog's training in order to compete at Working Tests or Field Trials.

Training classes with experienced instructors are invaluable in achieving your aims. Informative books are available on Gundog and Obedience training and can be fully comprehensive as they are written by experts in their field. Videos on the subjects are now available, and these can give a new perspective to teaching, as all the exercises are demonstrated visually.

OBEDIENCE

Obedience training classes are normally separated into classes for pet training, and classes for those who want to get involved with competitive Obedience. The novice exercises are ideal for both dog and owner, giving a good groundwork in basic obedience. Classes are held on a group basis, which helps

Control is an essential part of all training. This working Springer is learning to walk on the lead.

TEACHING THE RETRIEVE

The Springer must wait until the command is given before he goes out to retrieve.

A clean pick-up and a swift return to the handler is called for. The dummy must be released on command.

your dog to concentrate, despite the distraction of other dogs – and it also makes for an enjoyable social occasion for you.

If your puppy quickly masters the basic training, you can advance to formal training, which includes such advanced exercises as Retrieve, Scent Discrimination and Heel off-lead. When you feel you have reached a satisfactory standard, you can take the plunge and enter obedience competitions, commencing with the novice classes scheduled at these events. The transition is then to move into the higher ranks and compete in the advanced classes.

Obedience tests are sometimes held in conjunction with all-breed and breed (Specialty) shows. Obedience shows are also run by training clubs, catering solely for the Obedience competitor. There are a number of awards to work towards, and if your dog is highly successful he could become an Obedience Champion, or you can work towards the titles of Companion Dog (CD), Utility Dog (UD), Working Dog (WD) and Tracking Dog (TD), which graduate in degrees of difficulty. Regardless of what level you reach in competition, you will find that an obedience trained dog is a pleasure to live with, as good manners and agreeable behaviour are a way of life.

AGILITY

This sport was invented in the UK in 1978, and it has now become popular worldwide, and, along with Flyball, is considered to be a fun event – although it is highly competitive at the top level.

An Agility course consists of a series of obstacles, which your dog has to negotiate on your commands. The obstacles include a variety of hurdles, an A-frame, a dog-walk, a see-saw, a tunnel, a long jump and a tyre. This is where the training in basic obedience can prove worthwhile, as your dog will be working off-lead.

The course is set against the clock, and this can be the downfall of the speedy, fun-loving Springer, who will collect faults if he fails on the 'contact points' marked on the obstacles. However, as long as both handler and dog are fit and enjoy Agility competitions, this sport can serve to develop a close rapport.

GUNDOG TRAINING

The English Springer is of ancient lineage, and was originally bred to work with the falconer and Greyhound in springing the game. Hence, the name Springer. Today, it is his task to find, flush and retrieve game for the gun and, as such, all training should be conducted to satisfy these natural instincts. Although basic obedience and the elementary gundog exercises are the basis of a good worker, nothing can replace your local gundog club which will run training classes where you will receive the expertise and wisdom of trainers well-versed in this work.

Equipment will be required and your normal 'starter pack' will consist of: a whistle (not the pea type), a good nylon or rope slip-lead, two canvas covered land dummies (a cork-filled dummy for use in water, and an improvised dummy of an old stuffed sock or glove to teach a puppy to retrieve). These items may be on sale at your local club, or they may be available from sporting goods mail order catalogues.

FIRST LESSONS

Early training can commence at home, with the simple retrieving of a rolled up glove. Use the hallway or a corridor, and position yourself to be in your Springer's line of return. If he runs off with the dummy, never chase him but walk away and let him follow you. When your puppy comes to your call, do not grab at him. Wait a moment before taking the dummy. Gently open his mouth and take the dummy, saying "Dead", and praise him for delivering to hand.

Puppies should be acclimatised to noises, such as loud bangs, rattling of feed bowls, hand-clapping, etc. in preparation for the introduction of gunfire. You will need to use a starter pistol, firing blanks, and walk a distance from your puppy. Always raise the pistol arm in the air, using the command "Sit" as you fire. Gradually decrease the distance, always using the command "Sit" until your pup is steady. Hopefully, there will be no problems when it comes to the real thing.

A puppy should be taught to respond to verbal commands and to the whistle. If the whistle is used after a command, the puppy will soon respond to the whistle note. Whistle signals vary with trainers, and can be one or several notes, associated with the various exercises. The whistle should be introduced gradually until each whistle command is understood by your puppy.

An important lesson is to teach your puppy not to chase game or livestock. If he shows this tendency, the use of a rabbit pen with natural cover in it can quickly quash his misdemeanours. Put your puppy on a long cord and let him run about in the pen, using his natural hunting instincts. Once a rabbit is put up and runs out from the cover, the pup will probably try to chase it. This must be stopped immediately, either by using the whistle or giving the command "Sit".

If your puppy obeys your command, give him lots of praise and call him back to you. If your dog persists in chasing the rabbit, then it is back to square one until he is reliable and retrieving dummies from the pen, ignoring the rabbits. Now that he is steady and reliable in the pen, you can progress to cold and shot game.

You can also teach your puppy quartering by training him to work systematically in a zig-zag fashion, covering the area ahead of you. Whistled signals will be used at regular intervals, so as not to disturb any game. Using hand and whistle signals, you will be able to control your dog by directing him left or right until, after practice, you will be able to walk in a straight line with your Springer working ahead.

By about six or seven months of age, your puppy's confidence will have

A typical day's pheasant shooting in the English countryside, with English Springers lined up ready for a work.

The Springer, pictured here retrieving pheasant, is an asset to any sportsman.

This highly intelligent breed can also be trained as drug detection or 'sniffer dogs', and a number are used by Customs and Excise in Britain.

developed, and, according to his development, more advanced training can be attempted. Providing the obedience and simple elementary retrieving exercises have been absorbed, then all should augur well for the puppy. A steady pup can now advance to retrieving hidden dummies, retrieving from water, and be taught to jump fences. If you are unsure about your puppy and feel he may be a little headstrong, it might be a good idea to start by taking him to some organised shoots where he can be employed picking up after each drive.

FIELD TRIALS
If you wish to enter for Field Trial competition, you must be confident that both you and your dog have reached an acceptable level of competence. For a first-timer it can be a nerve-wracking experience; you will be competing against dogs whose standard has been achieved by experience, knowledge and patience. Most Field Trial societies and clubs schedule different categories for beginners, such as Puppy and Novice stakes.

Spectators are welcomed at these events, and I advise you to spend a day just watching the dogs and handlers at work. During the close season, when there is no work to keep gundogs in training, many gundog Working Tests are organised. Although run on the same lines as a Field Trial, they consist of artificial exercises and, as they are held during the spring and summer, they can be social events with families organising picnics in the rural setting.

Chapter Five
ADULT CARE

GROOMING

Conscientious owners must ensure that their dog is groomed, as this is the process by which we care for his health, cleanliness, well-being and appearance. Regular grooming is essential, and when this is introduced as a routine, it takes little of your time. If you have acquired a show prospect puppy, it is beneficial to stand him on a table for a daily grooming session. This will keep the puppy's coat in good condition, and it will accustom him to being handled.

The show Springer is a judiciously trimmed breed, while the pet only requires trimming to the ears and feet. The correctly trimmed, well-presented, show Springer is a sculptured picture. If you require your dog to be professionally trimmed, it is best to contact a local Springer breeder. Grooming shops must be given specific instructions regarding trimming, as, in the normal course of events, electric clippers will be used – and in all probability, your dog will be returned with closely-cropped back and sides! Once a Springer's coat has been clipped it is almost impossible to restore to its original texture and condition.

For the purpose of show and general grooming, you will require good-quality equipment. This should include:

1. A fine-toothed, short-bladed steel comb.
2. A pair of straight-edged scissors.
3. A pair of 30-tooth thinning scissors.
4. A stripping knife and blades.
5. A wire hound glove with fabric back (to polish the coat).
6. A slicker brush (with steel-coated pins on one side).
7. Nail-clippers of the guillotine type.

Brushing and combing should be a daily task. Make sure you always work in the direction the hair grows. Take care with a steel-pin brush, especially on older dogs, as unseen lumps and abrasions can be scratched, sometimes drawing blood. This brushing and combing routine should clean out dead hair, and any seeds or thorns, etc., that accumulate in the coat during exercise.

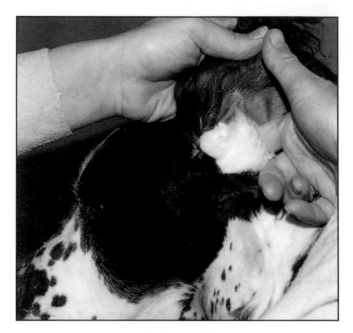

English Springers can be prone to ear problems, so make sure ear-cleaning is part of your regular grooming routine.

Nails should be trimmed regularly. This is a relatively simple task if you use guillotine cutters.

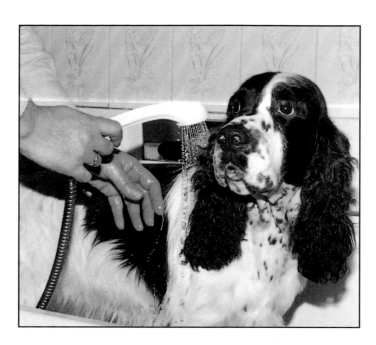

If you need to bath your Springer, make sure you use luke-warm water, and be careful that the water does not get into the ears.

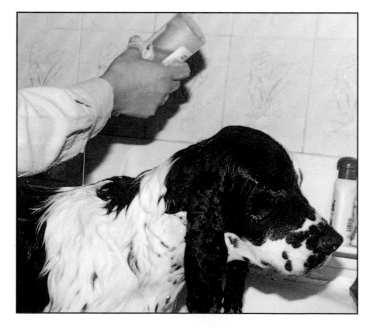

Use a canine shampoo and work into a rich lather. This must be rinsed off thoroughly before the dog is towelled dry.

EAR CLEANING

Springers are susceptible to ear problems as, due to their pendulous design, the ears do not permit the air to circulate in the ear canal. A check on the condition of the inner ear is an essential weekly chore. Ear-drops, available from the vet, should be administered, and cotton-wool or cotton-buds should be used to clean the outer section of the ear canal. Evidence of brown wax or putrid smells will indicate that your Springer may be suffering from ear mites or fungi. Every three months, it pays dividends to trim excess hair from the inside of the ear flap and the canal to allow air to circulate.

TEETH AND GUMS

Teeth and gum massage should be undertaken twice a week. Use an ordinary bristle toothbrush in a rotary motion. The brush can be dipped in a warm, saline solution, or a canine toothpaste can be used. Do not use human toothpaste, as it may contain substances which your dog is allergic to. If tartar accumulates, this can be scraped off by a vet, or you can purchase a tooth-scaler and learn to do this yourself.

EYES

Eyes should be bright and clear, so check for any signs of irritation from foreign bodies or from eyelashes. If a dog has problems with his eyes, he will probably try to scratch or rub at them with his paws. There may also be evidence of tear-stains.

FEET

Care of the feet and nails must be undertaken on a regular basis. The hair on the foot should not be allowed to grow too long between the toes and the pads as thorns, grass-seeds, and other foreign bodies can be hidden in them. Summertime is a high-risk period when the common grass-seed is in abundance.

The barbed seed heads can enter the dog's body, usually through the ears or the feet. A grass-seed left in the foot will disappear and make your dog lame. It is a matter of urgency that a vet removes the seed, as it can travel through the body and be potentially life-threatening if it reaches the vital organs.

To keep the feet clean and tidy, trimming, using the straight-edged scissors, should be carried out as necessary. With the dog standing still, hold the foot firmly, raise the hair between the toes towards you, against the grain, and cut downwards. On the outside of the paw, shape the foot, and neatly trim the hair level with the pad. Lift up the foot, and cut the hair level with the bottom of the pad. Dogs who are road-walked or exercised on concrete can wear their nails down to the correct length, but most dogs will need to have the nails clipped occasionally. This thought can strike dread into the pet owner, who fears he may injure the dog. However, with the guillotine nail-cutter it can be a simple operation. Nails have a quick, or nerve ending, and the cut must be made above this nerve. If you cut into the quick and cause bleeding, a dab of powdered coagulant will soon stem the flow.

BATHING

A well-groomed dog, who is brushed and combed daily, does not require frequent bathing. My advice is not to bath a dog unless you need to. Bathing tends to remove the natural oils and softens the coat. There can be exceptions, especially when your Springer has delighted in rolling on some noxious smelling waste!

If a bath is required, it is a wise precaution to have the towels and other necessities near to hand by the bath. Place a rubber mat on the floor of the bath to protect it from the dog's nails, and to prevent him from slipping. Use a canine shampoo, making sure you protect the eyes. Also try to avoid water entering the inside of the ears. Use lukewarm water to soak the dog, and rub in the shampoo. Rinse the dog thoroughly. When your Springer is ready to come out of the bath, throw a towel over him as he will most surely shake himself. Use several towels to make sure your dog is completely dry, and then gently brush and comb the coat. A hand-held hair dryer speeds this process, and makes for a handsomer result.

EXTERNAL PARASITES

During daily grooming, and especially after exercise, a close watch must be kept for signs of external parasites. A Springer's coat seems to be the ideal haven for them. Fleas cause a dog great irritation; they can be responsible for skin conditions and they are also an intermediary host for the tapeworm. An aerosol insecticide, available from the vet, will kill the fleas, and a thorough combing will remove the debris. Insecticides are also available to spray the dog's bedding and sleeping areas.

Other unwelcome visitors are lice. There are two kinds, the biting and the sucking louse. They are greyish-white in colour, and about the size of a pin-head. Once established, usually around the edges of a Springer's ear, they can quickly spread, causing intense discomfort to the dog. Lice can be eradicated using the same methods as for fleas, although several treatments may be required.

Ticks feed upon the blood of their host. The tick buries its mouth part into the dog's skin, enlarging in size as it sucks, and changing colour to purple. Do not attempt to pull off the tick as it is difficult to dislodge, and the head could stay in the skin and turn septic. The most effective method of removal is to dab turpentine on the body of the tick, and then to pull it out, using tweezers, after it has released its hold.

Harvest mites are prevalent during the summer months. They are distinguished by their orange/red colouring. Another irritant, they attack between the toes, inside the thighs and other areas, causing a rash. Treatment is a good veterinary wash.

A picture of health and fitness: The English Springer Spaniel thrives on a routine of regular exercise, good food, and careful attention to grooming.

THE VETERAN

Around twenty years ago, many Springers had a short lifespan of only eight years or so. The reason for this has never been satisfactorily explained. The breed now seems to be enjoying longevity, so your final responsibility is caring for your dog during the ageing process, which can take place from seven years onwards. In many ways, the signs of ageing are similar to those experienced by humans.

The older dog requires more security, more love, and more attention. The digestive system can present problems. It is therefore beneficial to feed your dog twice a day, so as not to burden the digestive system too much. It is equally important to avoid obesity. Exercise should be self-regulated according to your dog's age and inclination.

Daily grooming is of more importance, as nails will grow longer with reduced exercise, and the coat will require attention so that the dog is clean and comfortable. Above all, the older dog's requirements are to be kept warm, dry, and to have draught-free sleeping quarters. Minor ailments may arise, and in some cases, more serious problems may develop. If this happens, you should be guided by your vet, who has probably known the dog during his lifetime.

The fateful day will arrive when you may find your loved one has passed away in his sleep, when the body was at its lowest ebb. Or, when the quality of life has gone, you may have to make the difficult and painful decision of opting for euthanasia, in order to save your dog from further suffering. This is a heartbreaking time. I always cradle the dog in my arms when the vet sends him to sleep, so that the dog feels loved right to the end.

Many owners like to bury their pets in the garden. I now use cremation, when the ashes are returned in a wooden casket. If I ever move house, I know the casket will go with me, so that I can remember all the fun, affection and companionship I received over the years.

Chapter Six
THE SHOW RING

THE BREED STANDARD

Each breed has a descriptive written Standard, officially laid down by its parent breed club and approved by its national Kennel Club. The Standard defines the qualities and essential features that breeders should try to produce, and gives a blueprint for judges assessing the breed. The English Springer Spaniel Standard evolved in 1885, when the responsibility of compiling a Standard lay in the wisdom and experience of a group of working enthusiasts. It speaks volumes that this Standard, drawn up to fit a working Springer, is the accepted criteria of the show dog – and there have been very few amendments to the Standard over the years.

All countries are governed by the relevant Kennel Clubs who enforce the rules and regulations. The Federation Cynologique Internationale (FCI) now encompasses most of Europe and many far-flung countries of the world. Although the British Kennel Club is not a member of this organisation, the FCI ensures that any Breed Standards adopted under their jurisdiction originate from the land of origin. The Springer's country of origin is England and, as such, the British Standard is adopted.

The American Kennel Club is the ruling body in the USA but the English Springer Spaniel Field Trials Association is the guardian of the Standard. There is little difference between the American and British Standards, although I much prefer the American version, which is far more detailed.

The Standard is a guide to protect and preserve the breed characteristics, and to safeguard these qualities from becoming diminished or lost to the breed. The aim of the breeder is to strive for perfection according to the Standard. The perfect dog has not been bred, although Ch. Salilyn's Condor on his Westminster success was given the accolade by the Best in Show judge of "the nearest to perfection I have seen".

GENERAL APPEARANCE

The English Springer should present a balanced appearance in every part, free from exaggeration and well-proportioned. This medium-sized, sporting dog has a neat, compact body, and a coat of moderate length, with feathering on the ears, legs, chest and brisket. With his pendulous ears, soft gentle expression,

sturdy build, and friendly wagging tail, he is unmistakably a member of the
Spaniel family. The Springer's carriage is proud and upstanding, the body is
deep, and the legs are strong and muscular. Overall, the English Springer
suggests power, endurance, agility, and he is endowed with style and
enthusiasm. He is every inch a sporting dog, combining beauty and utility.

CHARACTER
The character and temperament of the English Springer is that of an extrovert
nature, and his friendly, happy disposition has endeared him to dog lovers in all
walks of life. Timidity or aggression is highly undesirable, and totally out of
character in the breed.

HEAD
The Springer's head should be impressive without being heavy. Its beauty lies
in a combination of strength and refinement. It is important that the size and
proportion be in balance to the rest of the dog. The skull is of medium length,
fairly broad, flat on top, and slightly rounded at the sides and back. The occiput
bone (the back point of the skull) is inconspicuous and rounded.
   The foreface is approximately the same length as the skull. As the skull rises
from the foreface, it makes a brow or moderate stop, divided by fluting
between the eyes. The stop, eyebrow and chiselling of the bony structure
around the eye sockets contribute to the Springer's beautiful and characteristic
expression. Nostrils are well-developed. Flesh-coloured (Dudley) noses are
undesirable.

EYES
More than any other feature, the eyes contribute to the Springer's appeal.
Colour, placement and size influence expression and attractiveness. The eyes
are of medium size and almond-shaped. They are set well apart and deep in
their sockets. The haw (the third eyelid in the inside corner of the eye) must not
show. The desired colour is dark hazel. An eye that is yellow or brassy destroys
the Springer's melting expression.

EARS
The correct ear set is on a level with the line of the eyes; on the side of the
skull and not too far back. The ears should hang close to the cheeks, and the
flaps should be long and fairly wide, with no tendency to stand up or out. The
leathers (the flap of the ear) should be approximately long enough to reach the
tip of the nose.

MOUTH
In order to carry game easily, the jaws should be of sufficient length, fairly
square, lean, strong and even. The upper lip should come down full and rather
square to cover the line of the lower jaw. The teeth should be strong and sound

The show scene in America: Am. Ch. Salilyn's Condor, rated "near to perfection" by the Westminster Best in Show judge.

The show scene in Britain: Sh. Ch. Penygader Chrystal Star. Note the difference in the way the English Springer is presented for the show ring.

The judge has to assess each dog in relation to the Breed Standard, which is a written picture of the 'ideal' Springer.

When a dog is on the move, the judge can evaluate gait, and the overall conformation of the dog.

with a perfect, regular scissor bite, i.e. the upper teeth closely overlapping the lower teeth, and set square to the jaws.

NECK
The neck should be of good length, muscular, slightly arched at the crest, and gradually blending into sloping shoulders. A Springer should not be noticeably upright in shoulder, as this will affect his movement. The neck should be clean and free from throatiness.

FOREQUARTERS
Efficient movement in front calls for proper, well set back shoulders. This permits the dog to swing his forelegs forward in an easy manner. Elbows should be close to the body, with free action from the shoulders. Forelegs should be straight and well-boned, and the pasterns (the region of the foreleg between the wrist and the digits) should be short, strong and flexible.

BODY
The body should be well coupled, strong and compact. The chest should be deep with well-sprung ribs, and the back should be straight and strong and practically level. The topline should slope very gently from the withers (the highest point of the body) to the tail.

HINDQUARTERS
The Springer should be shown in hard, muscular condition. Well-developed in hips and thighs, the whole rear assembly should suggest strength and driving power. The hocks (the group of bones on the hindleg forming the joint between the second thigh and the metatarsus) should be moderately angulated. When viewed from the rear, the hocks should be parallel whether the dog is standing or in motion.

FEET
The feet should be round and compact, with strong full pads. Excess hair should be removed to show the natural shape and size of the feet.

TAIL
The Springer's tail is an index both to his temperament and his conformation. A merry tail action is characteristic. The proper set is somewhat low, and it must never be carried above the level of the back. The carriage should be nearly horizontal.

GAIT/MOVEMENT
The Springer's movement is strictly his own. The forelegs swing straight forward from the shoulder, throwing feet well forward in a free and easy manner. The hocks drive well under the body, following in line with the

forelegs. In judging the Springer, there should be emphasis on proper movement which is the final test of a dog's conformation and soundness. Prerequisite to good movement is balance of the front and rear assemblies. The two must match in angulation and muscular development if the gait is to be smooth and effortless. Good shoulders, laid back at an angle that permits a long stride, are just as essential as the excellent rear quarters that propel the driving power. Seen from the side, the Springer should exhibit a good long forward stride, without high stepping or wasted motion.

COAT
The Springer is nicely feathered on the ears, chest, legs and belly. The hair is short and fine on the head, the front of the forelegs, below the hocks, and on the front of the hindlegs. The body coat is flat or wavy, and sufficiently dense to be waterproof, weatherproof and thornproof. The coat should have a clean, live appearance, indicative of good health. Although the appearance should be natural, it is legitimate to trim the head, feet and ears, and to thin and shorten excess feathering from the hocks to the feet and elsewhere, as required.

COLOUR
All of the following combinations of colours and markings are acceptable: liver and white, liver and white with tan markings (usually found on the eyebrows, the cheeks, the inside of the ears, and under the tail), black and white, and black and white with tan markings.

SIZE
The approximate height of the English Springer is 20 inches (51 cms). The American Standard takes a more sensible approach, with the ideal shoulder height for dogs being 20 inches, and 19 inches for bitches. The American Standard also states that a dog in good condition should weigh approximately 49-55 lbs. The Springer is built to cover rough ground with agility, reasonable speed and endurance, and he should be kept to a medium size.

SUMMARY
The Breed Standard attempts to outline the points of a good specimen. There can be a great variation in the way judges and breeders interpret the Standard, and this makes it all the more interesting. As long as there is no deviation towards exaggeration and all points are adhered to, the aim of the breed's enthusiasts will be satisfied by breeding appealing, typical English Springers.

SHOWING YOUR SPRINGER
Most devotees of the show world have first become involved either through accident or design. It may be that your dog has been admired at training classes, or perhaps the breeder feels the dog has sufficient quality to succeed in the show ring. There is, of course, the person who has specifically acquired a

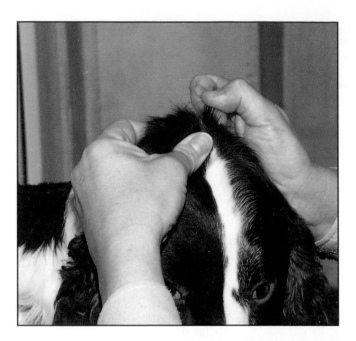

THE ART OF TRIMMING

The finger and thumb method can be used to pull out the longest hairs.

Trim the hair on the outside of the ears always working against the natural lie of the hair.

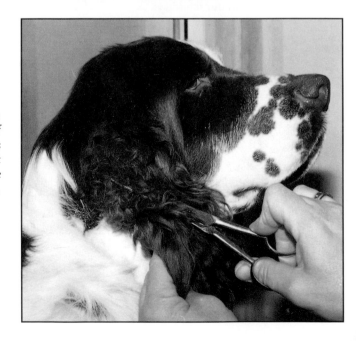

Trim the inside of the ears so that they lie flat.

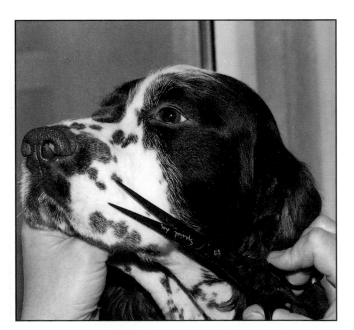

Tidy the muzzle, so that it looks neat and smooth.

puppy for show purposes. Before embarking on showing, you should be aware of several qualities that are desired in you as an owner. Sportsmanship is paramount, and you must be able to take criticism of your dog. The human element in dog judging may mean that your dog is one judge's 'cup of tea' and another's poison. A sense of humour is desired, and impeccable conduct at shows towards fellow exhibitors and judges is essential.

Financial reward can be discounted, but showing dogs can be an exciting hobby. If you last the course, you will build up relationships with fellow exhibitors and make life-long friendships. You may have a flair for exhibiting and breeding, and progress to becoming a successful breeder, exhibitor and judge. It will not be a fair assessment if you attend one show and become discouraged if you are unplaced. You will almost certainly be nervous, and this will pass down the lead to the dog. The whole structure of dog showing will be alien to you, but after a couple of outings it could be your day, and you return home a proud and happy winner.

Learning about the Springer is part of the apprenticeship, and the seasoned exhibitor or breeder will readily impart their knowledge to a newcomer. Above all, dog showing is a hobby and should be fun – the memory and thrill of your first prize or rosette will stay with your forever. However, you may rue that prize, as you will find that almost certainly you will have been bitten by the 'show bug', and you will be on your way to becoming a lifer!

SHOW TRAINING

If you have a puppy, training for the show ring should commence early. Most exhibitors 'top and tail' in the show stance. This is where the head is held in one hand, and the tail is gently supported in the horizontal position by the other hand. The dog should stand in a four-square position. Practise this with your puppy standing on a table, using the command "Stand". Gradually, your puppy will stand for longer periods, and this is the ideal time to ask friends to gently handle the pup, especially in areas like the mouth and hindquarters, to prepare him for examination by judges. It is beneficial to take your puppy to ring training classes where he will be taught the disciplines required in the show ring, and will encounter some of the noise and atmosphere associated with the show world.

There are different types of shows, ranging from the informal to the Championship Shows, where dogs compete at the highest level. It is a good idea to start off in the more relaxed atmosphere of a smaller show, and graduate to Championship level when you, and your dog, have learned the art of showing.

Dog showing is increasingly becoming a family outing. Many parents encourage their children to participate in the very popular junior handling or junior showmanship classes. The juniors have their own organisation and classes are judged on handling, not on the quality of the dog. I am a great advocate of these competitions as they encourage the Juniors to have pride in their appearance, the self control and discipline of the dog, good manners and sportsmanship. After all, they are the generation of the future. The standard of junior handling can be so high as to put most of the senior exhibitors to shame!

PREPARING FOR A SHOW

Hopefully, your early training will now be paying dividends You will have a dog who will be reasonably well-trained to stand, and will allow a judge to go over him. Your Springer should also be able to move on a loose lead, with a lovely natural, free-moving gait. You will want your dog to be in the peak of condition, and he should also be trimmed and groomed to the best of your ability. It is natural that a novice is apprehensive of trimming, as a badly trimmed Springer can take months to recover his coat.

Trimming should take place about a week before the show. The 'finger and thumb' method, holding the skin between the thumb and forefinger of one hand, and pulling the tips of the longest hairs with the other hand can prove to be laborious and very time consuming. A combination of 'finger and thumb' with the use of thinning and straight-edge scissors is generally more acceptable.

Starting with the head, remove any long tufts of hair on top by finger and thumb, plucking until the appearance is smooth and tidy. Using trimming scissors, trim the hair on the outside of the ears approximately one-third of the way down, until smooth. Always use the trimming scissors against the natural lie of the hair, continually combing out. Inspect the results before resuming. Trim out the underside of the ear to make it lie flat to the head.

The Springer should be clean in throat, so trim the hair from under the chin to the brisket bone. Thin the shoulders and blend the hair into the body. Using straight-edged scissors, trim the hair to the shape of the feet. Cut around the pads, and cut the hair from between the toes by brushing the hair up. Hold the toes together and trim the hair evenly. Cut the excess hair from the underside of the foot. On the front feet above the rear of the pad, trim the hair back to the 'bobble' or stopper pad until it is smooth. Remove hair from the back hocks, trimming close till smooth. Trim the long hair off the tail so that it appears rounded and neat. Thin out the hair around the anus to form a triangular shape. Any dead hair on the back or flanks can be taken off, using the finger and thumb method.

This is a rough guide to the art of trimming your Springer. If you are still hesitant, you should consult an expert groomer or breeder. If for some reason your dog requires a bath, this should be carried out the day before the show. Leave your dog slightly damp and put a coat or towelling on him. This will keep your dog's coat nice and flat and prevent 'fluffing'. Try to keep the towelling on the dog until you reach the show, and then you can give a quick brush, hopefully ending up with a flat, gleaming coat.

On the eve of the show, it is a good idea to prepare your show bag. This should include your grooming equipment, a couple of nylon show leads, and a bottle of water (it is sometimes a long trek to a tap). Your dog should travel to

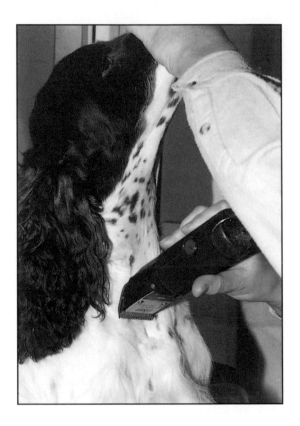

LEFT: The Springer should be clean throated. This can be trimmed using scissors or with a trimmer

BELOW: The coat must be combed through so that it is lying flat and smooth to the body.

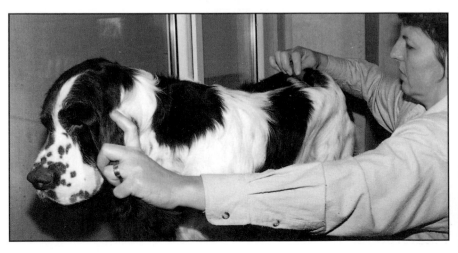

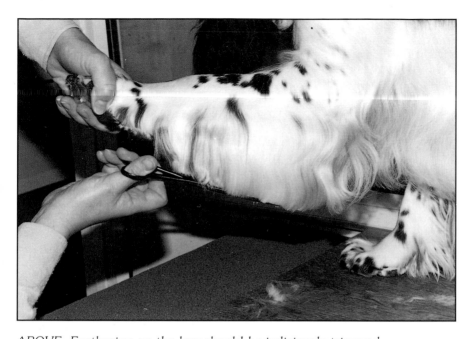

ABOVE: Feathering on the legs should be judiciously trimmed.

BELOW Trim the long hair from the tail so that it appears rounded and neat.

the show in his crate, which will also be a safe haven at the show venue. In the UK, Championship shows are benched, so you will require a benching collar and chain. A piece of carpet or blanket will help your dog settle on the bench. Do not forget your pass or schedule, and make sure you wear suitable and comfortable clothing. So, with your dog in fine fettle and looking spick and span, you are all ready to catch the judge's eye!

YOUR FIRST SHOW

At the break of dawn, nerves should have you up bright and early. Try to leave on time, making allowances for traffic hold-ups and the inevitable delays at the showground.

When judging commences, make sure you are already outside the ring until your class is called by the ring steward – the greatest asset to judge and exhibitor alike. The steward will assist and direct you in the ring procedure required by the judge. On entering the ring, do not amble or slouch with your dog but smartly show him. The judge may appear to be nonchalant, but you may impress him on the initial entrance. The steward will organise the exhibitors in a line, and, as a novice, you are advised to be near the end of the line, so you can watch the proceedings. It is usual practice to stand your dog in the show position during which time the judge will walk down the line, assessing the overall picture of the dogs.

After this examination, you may be asked to move around the ring. Keep your dog on the left, as this is the side normally on view to the judge. At this stage, the judge will be assessing toplines and side movement, which, in our breed, means showing plenty of driving power. The dogs will then be called forward for individual examination. This will entail checking each dog, assessing the head, mouth, ears, eyes, and body – the conformation of the dog.

When it is your turn, stand your dog and put the lead loosely over his shoulders. As the judge examines your dog, you can move to the rear as he goes over the front and vice versa, always accentuating the good points of your dog. The judge will then ask you to move your dog, either straight up and down or in a triangle, in order to assess the dog's rear and front action. You can now return to the line of dogs and relax those knocking knees!

However, do not relax too much. You must ensure that your dog is always looking his best, as a judge who likes your dog can still be stealing the occasional glance. The moment of truth comes when you are requested to stand your dog for the judge's selection. It is customary to award a number of placings, and then to give the prize card to the winning dog. In the ring, it is frowned upon to converse with the judge, but it is quite in order to approach him after judging to offer thanks, and also to obtain his opinion of your dog.

Chapter Seven
BREEDING ENGLISH SPRINGERS

With the upsurge of demand for bitch puppies over the last decade, it is natural to assume that more owners would eventually like to breed a litter from their bitch. There can be many reasons for the novice to want to breed a litter – friends and relations may admire your bitch and would like to own a dog just like her, or you want to breed a puppy to carry on the family line. No matter what the reason, you will find breeding a litter satisfying, interesting, pleasurable and one of the most exciting aspects of keeping dogs. However, the novice is cautioned that breeding dogs should never be regarded casually. You must take the ultimate responsibility for the dogs you have brought into the world.

TO BREED OR NOT TO BREED
Until recently, you may have received advice to breed from a bitch because it would benefit her health and well-being. However, advances in modern veterinary science mean that drugs have been developed, which end worries and problems regarding the womb and reproductive organs. Now an owner can breed a litter if he or she wants to, and can even plan the litter so that the puppies are born at the best time of year.

An unregistered bitch must not be bred from, as the puppies cannot be registered. You will also find that any reputable breeder will not allow their stud dogs to be used with such bitches, or even with registered bitches of pet quality.

Do not expect to make a fortune out of breeding a litter – it can be an expensive business when you take the stud fee, the veterinary fees, the food, and advertising into consideration. It can also be extremely time-consuming. Dependent on the size of the litter, you can run at a loss, or the best you can expect will be to break even.

THE BROOD BITCH
Most pet owners obtain a puppy purely for the Springer temperament, with looks as a secondary consideration. In their minds, these are qualities that they hope the bitch will pass on to her offspring, because the puppies are generally destined for pet homes. However, it is also important that the prospective

ABOVE: Don Miller picks out his show winners. Any dog used for breeding must be a typical representative of the breed, and be free from any inherited diseases.

RIGHT: The results of a well-planned breeding programme are self-evident.

ABOVE: This black and white bitch is from a working kennel. Her puppies are now one week old.

LEFT: The puppies' eyes will not open until they are about ten days old.

brood bitch is a good example of the breed, showing many of the associated breed characteristics. Above all, she should be physically healthy, and mentally sound, with no aggressive or nervous traits. She should be free of any hereditary diseases.

THE SEASON

A bitch normally comes into season twice, at six monthly intervals. This lasts for a period of three weeks or sometimes longer. Usually, a youngster will first come into season at the age of eight or nine months. The signs of a bitch coming into season include a swelling of the vulva, and the actual season will commence with the show of some spots of blood. This discharge is known as the first day of 'heat', and this will continue until the tenth or eleventh day when it will change to a clear discharge. This can be an indication that your bitch is ready to be mated. The bitch will indicate her willingness to be mated by turning her tail to the side when you tickle her just above the tail.

Never mate a bitch in her first season, as she is not physically or emotionally mature enough to cope with a litter. The second season onwards, or between eighteen months and three years, is the opportune time. When your bitch comes into season notify the stud dog's owners so that arrangements can be made to visit him. Mating can take place between the eleventh and fourteenth day, although there can be enormous variations to this. My advice to an owner bringing his bitch to be mated is to have her checked by a vet to ascertain whether she is ready, and to check that she is free from a stricture. This can be a tough membrane in the vagina that can prevent the stud dog from penetrating. It is advisable that this is attended to by the vet, and mating should be postponed until the next season.

THE STUD DOG

The breeder of your bitch will guide you as to the choice of a stud dog. This could be a dog with a complementary pedigree, but care should be taken that the dog is not too closely related. Dogs that are successful in the show ring or in the field may appeal to you, and you may feel that their reputation would assist in selling the puppies. However, it is more important that you like the dog, and you feel that he can produce good temperament and typical offspring. My advice would be to use an experienced dog, as mating two novices can be a haphazard experience.

THE MATING

It is customary to take the bitch to the dog. A worthwhile stud dog will soon tell you if the bitch is ready for mating. If he shows little interest, she is either too early or too late on in her seasonal cycle. If you are too early, it can mean return journeys to the stud dog until you fix on the correct day, or leaving the bitch as long as required.

With a maiden bitch, it is helpful to have a flirtatious dog who will encourage her to relax. Sometimes a bitch will require some lubrication to help the stud dog, and for this purpose I use a lubricant gel. To my cost, I have found that Vaseline can act as an anti-spermicide! Some bitches can be nervous or even aggressive when they are being mated. So, if you have a difficult bitch, you should use a muzzle. A make-shift muzzle, e.g. a pair of tights, tied around the head and muzzle, and under the chin will offer sufficient protection.

When the serious business of mating gets underway, you will probably be asked to give assistance by holding the bitch's head, while the dog's owner supports the bitch under the loins. Once the mating is achieved, there follows what is termed a 'tie'. This occurs when after the dog has passed the sperm, the penis swells and the dog and bitch are unable to release themselves. Although the dog may try to turn himself, the owner will usually assist him into the back-to-back position. This is to avoid any injury from occurring. A tie can last from ten to twenty minutes, during which time both dog and bitch must be held steady, as any attempt to pull away could result in physical injury.

Most owners like to see a tie, but a 'slip' mating can take place. This is where the dog enters the bitch for two or three minutes, without turning, and then withdraws. This does not mean that the mating has been unsuccessful. In fact, I know of large litters resulting from such matings.

After the mating, the bitch should be put in a quiet place and allowed to relax. As a season lasts for twenty-one days, all care must be taken to prevent an accidental mating. You must also ensure that you have completed all the paperwork required by the relevant Kennel Club. If your bitch fails to come into whelp, it is a courtesy of the stud dog owner to offer a free repeat mating at a later date. However, this is not a legal obligation, as the stud fee is paid for the service only.

THE PREGNANCY

A bitch can lead a perfectly normal life during the first three weeks of pregnancy, with the exception of being wormed about two weeks after mating. Until you are sure she is pregnant, do not increase her food or change her diet, although, I do introduce extra vitamin supplements at this stage. A bitch's pregnancy normally lasts sixty-three days or nine weeks. However, it is not until the fifth week that you may notice the first changes in behaviour, with the bitch slowing down and becoming more sedate. Ultrasound scan facilities are now available for bitches, but these are not infallible as Springer bitches can carry their puppies high in the ribcage and fool us all!

After about four weeks into the pregnancy, gradually increase the food intake with good nutritious food and the introduction of powdered milk, laced with a raw egg. By the seventh week, the bitch should be on two meals a day. Normal exercise is a necessity, but try to prevent jumping and any other frantic activity. During this time, the bitch can easily abort and absorb the puppies.

The sixth week will show positive, physical signs of pregnancy, with the teats enlarging, and the body shape changing and growing rounder. Now is the time

Weaning starts at around three weeks of age. These eight-week-old puppies are now fully independent from their mother.

Play is an important part of the puppies' early development.

A job well done! These two puppies are now ready to leave their mother and go to new homes.

to consider where the bitch is going to whelp and to get her accustomed to the area where she will give birth. A house dog will want to have her puppies in a favourite area in the household – the kitchen, the utility room, or even in the bedroom. A bitch who is accustomed to living outside will prefer an outhouse or something similar. All whelping quarters must have good lighting; they must be draught-free, and there should be an electric point for the use of an infra-red heat lamp.

A whelping box will be required, and this is easy to construct for any handy person. I suggest using tongue and grooved timber for the sides of the whelping box, with marine ply for the floor. The box should be large enough to accommodate the bitch lying on her side comfortably – the bitch's length, plus half her length again, would be correct. Overall size of the box should be 4ft by 4ft (1.2m by 1.2m). Three of the sides need to be 18ins high (46cms). The fourth side should be hinged and improvised as a ramp, so that the puppies can get in and out at a later date. You will need to build a wooden rail of 1-2ins all round the inside of the box, set about 3ins above floor level. This is to prevent the bitch lying on the puppies, as they can receive protection by sheltering under the rail. The bed should also be raised above floor level.

Newspapers are the best type of bedding during whelping, as they can be easily disposed of. After a couple of weeks, polyester fleece bedding is ideal, as moisture soaks through it, and it is machine-washable. An infra-red heat lamp should be suspended from the ceiling over the box. This can be adjusted in height in order to regulate the heat. The ideal temperature to maintain for a new-born litter is 75-80 degrees Fahrenheit (25 Centigrade).

A bitch can produce a day or two before the due date without undue harm. However, if she goes beyond the whelping date by two or three days, it would be advisable to call in the vet. I always inform the vet of any litter that is due, in case of unforeseen problems.

THE WHELPING
It is advisable to be prepared for the whelping, and you will need to gather together: a pair of straight-edged scissors, mild disinfectant, towels, cotton-wool, and hot water should be on standby. There can be many signs of the bitch approaching delivery. She may refuse food and milk, there may be a slight discharge from the vulva, and her temperature will fall three degrees Fahrenheit below the normal 101.5 F (38.5 C). Urination may increase, and the bitch often tears frantically at the newspapers in the bed. Restlessness and increased panting will indicate that a puppy is imminent.

A series of powerful contractions will force the first puppy down the birth passages. The forerunner of a puppy arriving is the appearance of a fluid-filled bag at the vulva. The bag will burst, releasing the fluid it contains. A puppy should appear shortly. If there is a considerable delay in the appearance of a puppy, the vet should be summoned.

Puppies are usually born head-first, but breech births do happen. This is where the puppy will be presented feet and rump first. With assistance, this should not pose a problem. A puppy is sometimes presented in a sideways position, or it may be lodged in an abnormal position in the passage. Immediate veterinary attention is required, and if the vet is unable to free the puppy, a Caesarean birth will be needed.

Each puppy is born in a membranous sac which the bitch will open with her teeth, nipping the umbilical cord near the navel. As the supply of oxygen is now cut off, she will lick the puppy vigorously to enable an air intake to the lungs. Springers are usually easy whelpers, with puppies arriving at ten to twenty minute intervals. A maiden bitch can soon be exhausted, and I have seen puppies arriving within a minute of each other, with the bitch seeming almost unaware of what is happening. This is when your assistance is required. You will need to break the sac, where the puppy's head lies, and clean any fluid or mucus away from the respiratory areas. With sterilised scissors, cut the umbilical cord about one inch from the puppy's navel. Give a brisk rub with a towel, and then return the puppy to the mother, who will continue with the maternal process. The bitch will eat the placentas, if allowed to do so, but there is no need for concern as this is nature's way of giving nourishment.

During the whelping, I keep the bitch liberally supplied with warm milk and glucose. The mother will clean and dry each puppy, who will then find a teat and start to suckle. A bitch will tell you when she has finished whelping – she will become calmer and more settled. At this stage, take her out on a lead to relieve herself. Then wash her rear end, and any other soiled area, with warm water. While she is away from the whelping box, dispose of the soiled newspapers, and line the box with clean bedding. This is also a good time to check each puppy, and find out the number of dogs and bitches.

Arrange with your vet to give the bitch an antibiotic injection. This helps to prevent infection, and an oxytocin injection will assist in contracting the uterus. For a few days, the bitch will pass loose, dark-coloured motions, but she will soon return to normal. For a couple of days after whelping, restrict the bitch to light foods, with plenty of powdered milk, supplemented with glucose, calcium tablets and extra vitamins. Not all problems encountered on a whelping can be generalised. An experienced breeder's phone number to hand is invaluable for ready advice.

WEANING AND EARLY INFANCY

Provided your bitch is well fed and supplied with plenty of milk, she will settle down happily to tend to the puppies. She will keep the bed clean, feed the litter, and attend to their every need until they are about three weeks of age. In English Springers, the removal of dew claws and docking of tails should be carried out at three days old. This should be done by a veterinary surgeon.

Puppies need heat, and a contented litter will be spread across the floor of the whelping box, and you will hear little noise from them. If the puppies cry, it is most likely that they are cold or the bitch could have a problem with the flow

An evenly-matched litter – the product of excellent rearing.

The experienced breeder assesses each puppy, posing them in show position.

of milk. The bitch should be having a large intake of high protein to create a good milk supply. Examine the milk glands daily. If any appear hard and swollen, then a massage with a warm cloth will usually start the flow again. If this does not work, contact your vet for advice.

When the puppies are about two weeks old, you will need to trim their nails with scissors. Puppies' nails grow extremely quickly, and they can easily scratch the mother and make her sore. Thereafter, the nails should be trimmed once a week. Puppies' eyes usually open from 10-15 days, and focus from three to four weeks. Hearing is fully developed by five weeks, and teeth begin to appear when the pups are about a month old. At four weeks old, the litter will be exploring the new world, tumbling in and out of the box. Puppies learn quickly and will soon understand how to use the ramp.

At about three weeks, the process of weaning can commence. Puppies should be taught to lap from saucers filled with warm, powdered milk. During the next week, the meals should be increased from one to four feeds daily. Meat should be introduced when the puppies are four weeks old. For this purpose, I still use saucers, and I provide small quantities of a special canned puppy food, which has been well mashed. I find this food is easily digested, and there is no risk of the puppies choking. There should be no problem with the introduction of meat because Springer puppies are greedy and messy little devils! Quantities of milk and meat should be gradually increased until, at five weeks old, the puppies will be on five meals a day. Two of milk and cereal, two of meat, and one milk meal. At five weeks, I would consider the puppies to be fully weaned.

As soon as weaning commences, the bitch will want to spend less time with the puppies, although she will still be feeding them. This is when you begin to wonder if it was all worth it – for now you have to clear up after the puppies, and commence the regime of feeding! With the milk drying up at about five weeks, the bitch will probably want to spend more time alone, giving the pups a final check before retiring.

Puppies should be wormed for roundworm at five weeks and seven weeks. I have found a paste wormer to be the most effective; it is palatable and easiest to administer.

Summer puppies are certainly the ideal puppies! I have a purpose-built run that can be moved about the garden, even though it leaves the lawn looking terrible! I put a bed in the run, and I always make sure that fresh water is available. I also put a board across the run to give the puppies shade. Many an idyllic and time-wasted afternoon has been spent just watching the puppies playing, and seeing how their individual characters develop. It is a most rewarding experience and, for the novice, it is a sad parting when the puppies leave to go to their new homes at eight weeks. You will have found breeding a litter to be an enjoyable and exciting venture – and you will have participated in one of the greatest wonders of nature.

Chapter Eight
HEALTH CARE

FINDING A VET
When you are acquiring a dog for life, you are also befriending a veterinary surgeon for life! This is what a vet should be – a friend to your dog and a confidant for you. A vet on twenty-four hour call-out is offering a service that can save your loved pet. It is important that you use the veterinary services for any problems with your dog that cause you concern.

FIRST AID
A first aid kit should be kept in the house, and in the car. This should be equipped to deal with minor, everyday problems that may be encountered. First aid is precisely that, so, if an emergency does occur, keep calm and use your commonsense. A first aid kit should include:

Cotton-wool (cotton)
Cotton-wool buds
Antiseptic disinfectant
Bandages (cotton and crepe)
Adhesive tape
A rectal thermometer
Antiseptic cream and powder
Absorbent tissues
A roll of kitchen paper
Scissors
Tweezers.

COMMON AILMENTS

ANAL GLANDS
A dog dragging its bottom along the ground can be associated with worms, but in Springers this behaviour is usually caused by an anal gland disorder, which can prove intensely irritating to the dog. The two anal glands are situated on either side of the anus and are used to assist the passage of faecal waste. These glands secrete a foul-smelling liquid that needs to be emptied for the comfort of

the dog, and to prevent abscesses forming. Take a large piece of cotton-wool and place it under the dog's tail. Gently squeeze upwards and together with your covered fingers. If you do this correctly, the liquid will be easily expelled. For obvious reasons, it is best to do this when the dog is being bathed.

BURNS AND SCALDS

Apply cold water to the affected area and let it soak. This will enable you to see how much of the skin has been affected. If the burn is extensive seek help from the vet. Small burns and scalds can be treated at home by applying a soothing lotion such as olive oil. Apply a penicillin cream to prevent infection. A resulting factor from burns and scalds can be shock. Ensure that your dog is kept warm, and do not give anything by mouth until you have sought professional advice.

CUTS

Minor cuts are normally licked clean by the dog, but deep cuts should be bathed in hot water and treated with an antiseptic disinfectant. If a cut looks really serious, it may require stitching. In this instance, cover the cut with cotton-wool, and bandage. Then take the dog to the vet. If an artery has been cut, put a tight bandage on a pressure point. If you are unsure about locating a pressure point, tie the bandage above the cut and tighten it to stop the bleeding. Loosen the tourniquet now and again, to allow blood to flow to the affected part. Take the dog to a vet as quickly as possible.

COPROPHAGY

This is a condition where the dog is addicted to eating his own faeces. Some claim that the cause is a vitamin or iron deficiency. There are many theories on how to curb this behaviour; most do not work. I have tried many remedies, and I have found the introduction of charcoal biscuits into the diet can assist.

MANGE

This condition is transmitted to dogs and humans from an infected dog or from the bedding of an infected dog. There are two types of this skin disease. The most common is sarcoptic mange, where the mite burrows under the skin and lays its eggs. It can be easily cured, but if it is left untreated, it can swiftly spread over the body causing nasty scabs. The second type is demodectic or follicular mange, which is not transmissible. The mite lives in layers of skin and can also affect the dog's glandular system. Severe irritation results and if the condition is not treated, abscesses can form. The tendency to contract this form of mange appears to be hereditary.

ECZEMA

This is an inflamed condition of the skin causing intense irritation. Fleas can cause an allergy, but skin irritations can be caused by other allergies. A process

RIGHT: From the moment your new puppy arrives, you are responsible for his health and well-being.

BELOW: Feed your Springer top-quality food, and make sure you never allow him to become obese.

The English Springer is an active dog and requires plenty of exercise.

of elimination must be used to find the cause, and so the best course of action is to seek veterinary advice.

POISONING
If you suspect, or know, that your dog has been poisoned, it is a matter of urgency to encourage him to vomit by administering a strong solution of salt and water. Call the vet immediately.

RINGWORM
This is a disease that can be transferred to humans. The signs are small, round patches on the skin resembling rings. It can be treated with modern remedies. Children must be kept away from an affected dog at all times.

STINGS
Wasps and bees are the usual offenders. A bee will leave a sting, which can be removed with tweezers. It is advisable to follow this up by applying a saline solution or antihistamine cream. Wasps do not leave stings, so simply apply a saline solution or antihistamine cream to the affected area. Stings can be dangerous if they are in the mouth or in the throat, so if you suspect your dog has been stung in either of these areas, consult a vet immediately.

TEMPERATURE
If your dog appears to be off-colour, but is showing no obvious symptoms, it is wise to take his temperature. The normal temperature for dogs is 101.5 degrees Fahrenheit (38.5 Centigrade). If the temperature has risen by two or three degrees, seek veterinary advice at once. To use the thermometer, smear a little lubricant on it and insert in the rectum for about an inch. No force is required. Hold it in place for one or two minutes, and then gently withdraw.

HEREDITARY DISEASES
All breeds suffer from hereditary diseases, and we are fortunate in English Springers to have a low number of breed-related ailments. Responsible breeders, who have tested their stock, have greatly reduced the number of affected dogs in their breeding programmes. There are three severe retinal (eye) diseases that can be inherited by the English Springer.

RETINAL DYSPLASIA (RD)
This disease has several forms, but the worst manifestations are extensive retinal degeneration or detachment. It is present at birth (congenital), and is inherited as a simple recessive. Thus, disease control is easy to apply, given the known method of inheritance and very early diagnosis. The presence of the disease can be confirmed at six to seven weeks of age. Recessive inheritance means clinically clear carriers exist, but these are identified immediately they produce affected puppies.

CENTRAL PROGRESSIVE RETINAL ATROPHY (CPRA)

This disease can occur at any age from 18 months onwards, but most affected dogs show signs of the disease by their sixth birthday. Fortunately, the peripheral vision is not lost, but affected dogs can be severely handicapped.

GENERALISED PROGRESSIVE RETINAL ATROPHY (PRA)

This disease makes its appearance between 12 and 30 months of age, and always causes blindness. Night blindness will often be noticed as the first indication of the presence of PRA, but opthalmoscopic examination will pick up very early cases before there are any associated signs. The disease is inherited as a recessive, therefore clinically normal carriers exist.

ENTROPION

This is an hereditary condition of the eye, where the upper or lower eyelids turn inwards. The eye weeps continuously and if left unattended, can cause damage to the cornea. A simple operation can correct the condition. Dogs and bitches who have been affected must not be bred from.

Conjunctivitis can be caused by dirt, dust and other substances affecting the eyelids. This inflammation can be cleared up using a veterinary eye ointment. Puppies with runny eyes must have the correct diagnosis.

HIP DYSPLASIA

Hip dysplasia is common to man and animals. Considered to be an hereditary problem, it can also be caused by over-exercising puppies when the bones are immature. This is a ball-and-socket problem, and the condition occurs where the head of the femur is flattened and will not fit into the socket of the pelvis. In severe cases, the head of the femur can slip out of the socket altogether, and cause extreme pain. This condition can cause lameness and peculiarities in the dog's gait. An X-ray is needed to reveal the true extent of the damage. If diagnosed, it is advisable not to breed from an affected animal.

FUCOSIDOSIS

Diagnosed in 1983 by Sydney University, Australia, this is essentially a human disease, and the British-bred English Springer is one of the few breeds to be affected by it. Fucosidosis is a fatal, inherited disease of the nervous system. It is incurable and can affect dogs and bitches. It usually affects young adult dogs between 18 months and four years old.

The symptoms include unexplained loss of weight, steadily worsening wobbliness of gait, loss of balance, change in voice, odd muscle spasms, apparent deafness, impaired vision, and increasing difficulty in swallowing. It is inherited through an autosomal recessive trait, and it is important to distinguish between clear, carrier and affected dogs. Clear dogs are those who neither have, nor carry, the disease. Carriers are those who show no signs of the disease, but are capable of producing carriers or affected offspring. Affected dogs are those who actually have the disease, and are the product of a mating between two carriers.

In 1985, Dr Bryan Winchester of the University of London was conducting research into the human side of the disease. On hearing the plight of the English Springer, he developed a simple blood test to identify dogs that are clear and those that are carriers or affected.